24 Hours To Share
What Really Matters

Before, During, and After COVID-19

Nicci Meadow

24 Hours To Share What Really Matters
Before, During, and After COVID-19

Text ©Nicci Meadow
www.niccimeadow.com

Design/Art Direction: LisaThompsonGraphicDesign.com
Cover Art: Hayden Shea-Meadow

Unless otherwise noted, all illustrations, photographs, etc. are courtesy of the author.

First printed 2020

Dedication

To Hayden Shea-Meadow — I love you always and forever — and in memory of Tracy Richards and Hugo "Holly" Hollerorth. I would like to express my appreciation and gratitude to Brett Peruzzi for editing, Lisa Thompson for designing this book during such unprecedented times, Hayden Shea-Meadow for the cover art and design, Jeff Alexander for my website, and Ayodele Johnson, Paula Krentzel, Lee Meadow, Marsha Zabarsky, and Gustavo Kinryas.

Contents

Preface

I originally wrote *24 Hours To Share What Really Matters* in 2017 after the death of a childhood friend who passed away six months after a pancreatic cancer diagnosis. A week later, a 93-year-old friend shared with me that no one alive knew his life stories to include in his eulogy or obituary. From these experiences I came up with the idea that an easy-to-use book could be very helpful for people to quickly write about their lives and what is important to them in a structured way.

With the COVID-19 pandemic, *24 Hours To Share What Really Matters* feels more relevant than ever, so I've modified it a bit for the current situation the world is facing.

Introduction

What are you going to do tomorrow? What's on your calendar? Don't turn the page. Take the next few minutes — no more than one or two — to think about it. Close your eyes if you want, and go through everything you have to or are planning to do tomorrow. Then turn to the next page.

What if all you had is tomorrow? Assume for now, that there will be no "day after tomorrow." "What?" you say. "Of course, there will be. There's always a tomorrow — and the day after tomorrow." And it's going to be sunny right? Maybe you know the song from the musical *Annie.* But for the purposes of this exercise let's assume there will not be a tomorrow for you.

Welcome to *24 Hours To Share What Really Matters.* Maybe you will have tomorrow, and maybe you won't. None of us really knows what's going to happen next.

Most of us go about our lives thinking we have all the time in the world. But who says? Most of us act as if we are not going to die — almost all the time. We are pretty unconscious, asleep, otherwise distracted most of the time. Maybe that's a good thing, maybe it's not. In the United States, most of us don't even want to look old — look at all those anti-aging products out there. Yet, at the same time, we walk or wheel around thinking we're going to get older, even old. We think we're going to have time to do that thing, or that other thing we've been wanting to do. We walk around like we're not going to die. We don't want to think about it — even as some of us are blowing up people on video games, watching movies and shows where people die in explosions or from other violence. But those aren't real people.

And if we're watching the news, it's terrorist attacks or bombings or a gunman at a concert, or gang killings. But if we're lucky, those are other people who are getting killed or dying. We have become immune, desensitized. We live in a death-denying country. So, whether we're 92 or 22 or 52, most of us don't want to think about dying. How we'll die or being dead. This project isn't actually about dying or how to die, or how to die a "good" death.

But that was before COVID-19. After the coronavirus spread around the world, and the U.S. is for now, leading the world in coronavirus cases, more of us — many Baby Boomers especially

— may be thinking about whether we will catch it and whether we might die as a result. We might think we know who is most at risk of dying from COVID-19, but we don't know the precise risk in any single subgroup. It's becoming known that in the U.S., those most at risk are people with low incomes and African Americans, Latinas, people of color.

We don't know when we will die — but the risk is 100% — each of us will die of something, some time. The coronavirus may or may not get otherwise young, healthy folks thinking too — though invincibility is prevalent in the minds of some of our privileged youth more immune from gun violence, or overdose, etc. There are some who may be secretly despairing, thinking what if ... It's not just the coronavirus, with hospital systems overrun and doctors and nurses overwrought, what we think of as run of the mill lifesaving treatments for heart attacks, gunshot wounds, and car crashes are going to be impacted, so we're all at risk, now more than ever.

This book is for folks who don't think they are going to die any time soon, and for those folks who are thinking they might in fact die, sometime sooner rather than later. It's for folks who have outlived most of their family and friends who knew them, or who just haven't shared a lot about themselves with friends or family, for one reason or another. It's for those folks who aren't thinking about dying at all, but who are seeking meaning in living their lives now, because they aren't as connected as they want to be, or their lives aren't as meaningful as they wish they were, or they don't want to face dying with regrets. Or they are out of touch with who they have become, and don't know who they are anymore, or they got so far away from who they thought they were, they don't even recognize themselves anymore.

It's for folks to start talking with others about what matters — or to leave a document or video for other folks who will write their obituaries. And though they're dead, they want it to say more than who their parents were, where they went to school, how long it took them to die, and where to send flowers or donations. It's also for people who care about each other to become closer. Because there are so few people who are willing or able to share their truths with us*, and not take them to their grave, so to speak.

There are a lot of religious and self-help books on mindfulness, impermanence, finding joy, gratitude, meditation, etc. One parable that boils it down to one sentence — is a Buddhist story of the little bird who sits on your shoulder every day and asks "Is today the day?" These books are all great — very intellectual, they talk the talk, but it's about walking the walk. You can read one book after another, lots of these authors are prolific — and they keep saying the same thing. Be here now. Breathe. Be mindful. But this is a book of questions, and you come up with the answers. Your own answers. Then if you are paying attention, and you really get it — that you, in fact, could die in 24 hours — you will do what you need to do, you will do what needs to be done, say what needs to be said, and you might die with fewer regrets — maybe. That's one of the goals of this book — to die with fewer regrets, achieve a few more of your dreams, get some dreams maybe, perhaps you had dreams you lost track of or didn't even know you had. Maybe you need to modify your dreams a bit, get a bit closer to the people you want to get closer to — or need to get closer to, or get away from the people who don't bring you joy or you don't bring joy to.

On the following pages you will find the guidelines for *24 Hours To Share What Really Matters*.

I suggest following them, but there really are few rules that absolutely everyone follows all the time; what's a rule anyway? If you want to change the ground rules, go ahead, but I can't guarantee the results. And I can't guarantee any results, because this isn't "evidence based". It hasn't been researched and tested, be-

*Adrienne Rich, *Women and Honor, Some Notes on Lying* (1975)

cause that would be expensive, and then there would need to be a control group, and "fidelity". And then some organization would probably copyright it, and sell it for a lot of money, and I'd hate that. But I appreciate it if you bought this book because I do need to make some money, not a lot of money, but enough money to cover the costs of producing it.

And if I make enough money, I'll give some of it away to a charitable organization in the U.S. I don't need recognition or fame, but if you like the book, and it works for you, and makes a difference in your life somehow, as it did in mine and countless others, I'll be satisfied. If it makes a difference, let me know, tell your story about *24 Hours To Share What Really Matters* on Facebook, YouTube, Twitter, Google Hangouts, Instagram, SnapChat, Pinterest, LinkedIn, TikTok or any other forum you use to communicate.

24 Hours To Share What Really Matters
– Guidelines –

- **You have 24 hours to live.** (Starting now — basically from the time you finish answering these questions — add an hour or two if you really need to.)

- **Over the next 24 hours your health — physical and mental — will remain exactly the same as it is right now**. You aren't going to gradually decline — you're not going to get sick, and you're not going to get better — you're just going to be how you are right now, but you will not be alive in 24 hours.

- **You can't physically travel** from the residence you are in right now to visit anyone and no one can come visit you.

[Before and after COVID-19, the following was the guideline: You can't travel more than 50 miles from your primary residence but your friends and family can come to you. You can take a train, plane, boat or automobile. Pretty much just your usual transportation. If flying or taking a train isn't typical for you, it's not really an option for purposes of this book. If you can't drive, someone else will drive you though, or you can take a bus or taxi. No more than 50 miles — not from your villa in France, or summer house on Cape Cod, or your cabin in the Vermont woods, but your primary residence — where you pay your taxes let's say, if you pay taxes. Where your dog, if you have one, is licensed. If there are friends and family you want to see more than 50 miles away, they can come to you. After COVID-19 — depending on what life looks like in the U.S., you can try out the pre-COVID-19 guideline.].

- **You have the material stuff that you have now.** There are no shopping sprees, you don't get any more money than you have now, you don't get to buy a big boat, or plane, and you don't even get to take that big trip you've been putting off. There's no granting of wishes. You don't get to meet your favorite celebrity.

- **You can't convert your assets or house or other real estate to cash to spend either.** You can't run up your credit card if you have one, and you can't spend all the money in your bank account(s) if you have any saved up — unless there is absolutely no one in your immediate family — blood or marriage — or someone like family, close friends included, who needs the money to live or they can get a lot more money easily without most of yours. I know what some of you are thinking, it's your money, you earned it, you're going to be dead in 24 hours, and you want to spend your money — like I said, there are no strict rules. Change the guidelines if you like, but I can't guarantee the results.

Now — on your mark, get set, go!

Go ahead and answer the following questions using the space provided.

I suggest writing your answers down but you don't have to. There are no "shoulds" in doing this or not doing this. If you want to write them down, write them down. If you can't write, ask someone else to write them down for you.

You don't need to write in sentences if you don't want to. You can just write down words, bullet points, or write an essay or a poem, or make a drawing. You can make a video of your answers and post it on social media or not. Take as long as you need, but not too long, because you may not get around to finishing it. Give yourself 15 minutes now, a half hour, an hour — whatever you can commit to doing. Write down something for each question; you can go back to it later if you really feel you need more time. Some of you won't even start — you'll put the book down now, and tell yourself you'll get to the questions later, when you have more time. But will you have more time? That's the big question for which no one has a definitive answer.

Few of us want to do this hard work. But ask yourself why aren't you going to start now. Take a look at the questions at least, and start thinking about them.

Remember that Rabbi Hillel (c. 110 BCE — 10 CE) famously said, "If not now, when? If I am not for myself, who will be? If I am only for myself, what am I?"

Then, after you answer these questions, do something on the list, at least start it, you don't need to finish it. Just take a step forward, since you never know what's going to happen next. Then do the next thing.

I suggest after you do *24 Hours To Share What Really Matters*, ask someone you care about to do it too, and agree to share your answers. Keep in mind that not everyone you share it with will do it or do it with you at the same time you do; that's okay. You can do it alone. It will make a difference in your life whether it's shared or not. You can share your answers in writing or when you get together virtually or in person whenever that might be, or email the answers. Or perhaps have a virtual gathering on Zoom, Skype or FaceTime and share your answer Together. Maybe you'll wear funny hats, have a drink, make it a party, or keep it serious. The sky is the limit. After you do *24 Hours To Share What Really Matters*, do it again next month; see what changed, and what didn't. Then maybe wait three months, and do it again. Repeat it again whenever you want.

24 Hours To Share What Really Matters
— Questions —

What will you do in the next 24 hours? List as many things or as few as you want — morning, afternoon, and evening. Be as specific as you want, in any time increments you want.

____

____

____

____

____

____

____

____

____

____

____

____

____

Who do you want to or would you want to spend time with and who will you do what with? If you can't be with them physically, think about who you would want to be with virtually too. Options include Zoom, Skype, FaceTime, SnapChat, text, phone, etc. Be sure to consider the person/people you are currently residing with.

If you could have traveled, where would you have gone? *Why is that place important to you? Before and after COVID-19: Where will you go? What will you do there? Why is that place important to you? Stay within 50 miles of your primary residence.*

____

____

____

____

____

What do you need to say? To whom do you need to say it?
Who: What you need/want to say: Why:

1. ____

2. ____

3. ____

4. ____

5. ____

6. ____

7. ____

8. ____

9. ____

10. ____

For each one, ask yourself why you haven't said it yet.
What are you afraid of if you said it? How do you think saying it will make you feel, and how the other person feels? What if you never get to say it?

____

____

____

____

What do you need to hear? And from who do you need to hear it?

Who   What   Why?

____

____

____

____

How do you think hearing it will make you feel?

____

____

____

____

What piece(s) of music/songs will you listen to or play?
On what instrument, if you play more than one?

____

____

____

____

____

What poem would you read, if you have a favorite?
Even if you don't want to read it in the next 24 hours, write
it down.

____

____

____

____

____

What favorite book would you read a passage from?
Even if you don't want to read it over the next 24 hours, write
it down.

____

____

____

____

____

What would you watch?

____

____

____

____

What sport would you play?

____

____

____

What prayer would you say or read if you have one?

____

____

____

What hobby would you engage in?

____

____

____

____

What would you eat and drink?

____

____

____

____

____

Later, if it's something you or someone else cooked, include the recipe. You can attach a photo or scan of that recipe or write it out.

What art, sculpture, painting, would you look at?
How does it make you feel and what do you see in it?

____

____

____

____

What art/craft would you make?

____

____

____

____

If you could tell others — your friends, family or strangers even — others who think they have more than 24 hours to live — what to try and change about the town/city, country you live in, or the world, what would it be and why?

____

____

____

____

What are you grateful for?

____

____

____

____

If you believe in God, or some other higher power, what might you say to that higher power in the next 24 hours?

____

____

____

____

What is one thing you haven't done, or seen, that you would do or see if you have another 24 hours, with the same guidelines as the last 24 hours?

____

____

____

____

What is one story you want to tell about your life or your experience that you don't think anyone alive now knows, or they know bits and pieces, or know it differently than you might have experienced it?

____

____

____

____

Where in the world was your most favorite place to be?

____

____

____

____

Where in your country and the world would you have liked to visit if you got the chance — beyond 50 miles from your primary residence?

What is one thing you would *not* do in the next 24 hours?

What advice would you give to someone, young or old, or in between, who is looking for advice? Whether it's a movie to see, a book to read, a place to go. Whatever you might have learned on this journey above ground that you want to pass on.

Other questions and answers you want to ask and answer for yourself.

1.____

2.____

3.____

4.____

5.____

**The next two questions are not required, but it could help
your friends or family.**

Do you have a will? ____

Have you named a guardian for your child(ren) if you
have them?

____

Do you have a health care power of attorney or proxy in case
you can't make health care decisions for yourself?

____

In your state, you can call your local bar association and get a
referral to a lawyer. Or call your doctor or local hospital for a
health care power of attorney form or health care proxy.

Notes